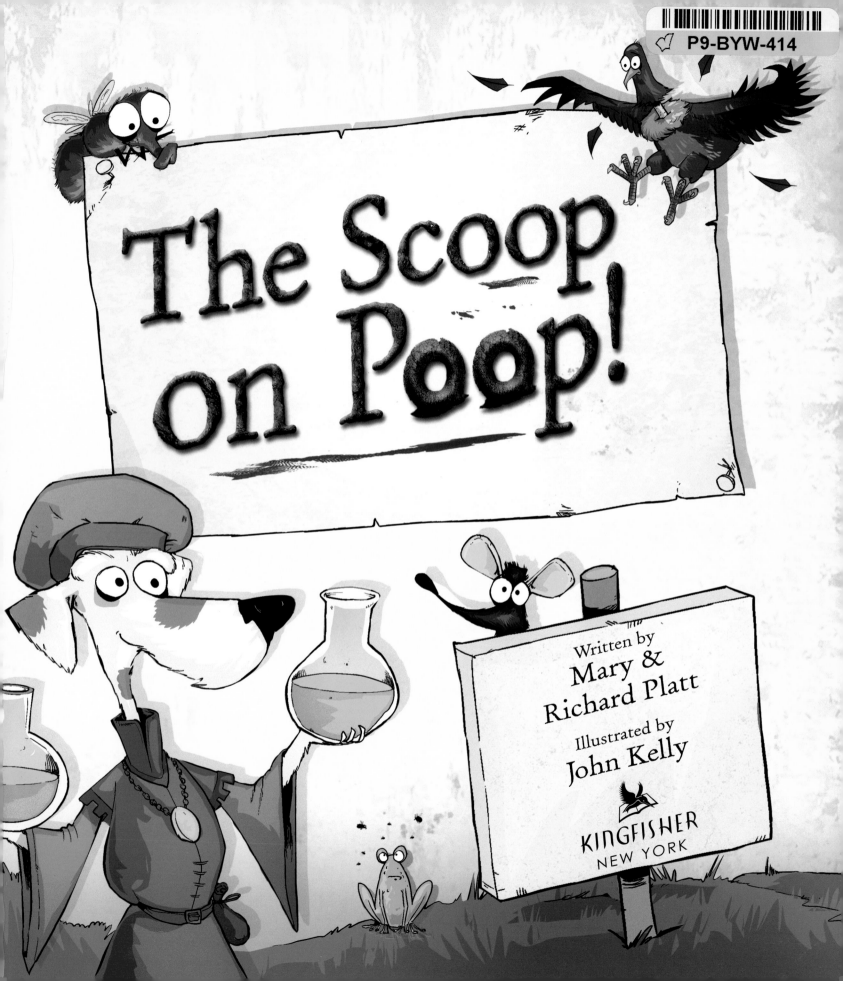

The Scoop on Poop!

Written by
**Mary &
Richard Platt**

Illustrated by
John Kelly

KINGFISHER
NEW YORK

KINGFISHER
LONDON & NEW YORK

Copyright © Kingfisher 2012
Published in the United States by Kingfisher,
175 Fifth Ave., New York, NY 10010
Kingfisher is an imprint of Macmillan
Children's Books, London.
All rights reserved.

Distributed in the U.S. and Canada by
Macmillan, 175 Fifth Ave., New York,
NY 10010

Dedicated to Austen

Consultant: Selina Hurley, Assistant Curator
of Medicine, Science Museum, London, U.K.

Library of Congress Cataloging-in-Publication data has
been applied for.

ISBN: 978-0-7534-6923-1

Kingfisher books are available for special promotions
and premiums. For details contact: Special Markets
Department, Macmillan, 175 Fifth Ave., New York,
NY 10010.

For more information, please visit
www.kingfisherbooks.com

Printed in China
1 3 5 7 9 8 6 4 2
1TR/0712/UTD/WKT/140MA

MEET THE POOP CREW!

CONTENTS

Roly
(a dung beetle)

Pecker
(a pigeon)

Buzz
(a bluebottle)

"Sniffer"Jenkins
(a dog)

Sidney Sewers
(a rat)

LUCKY
CHARMS

THE PEE AND

PART EXCHANGE
WELCOME!

PLOP SHOP

WAIT! Don't flush . . . not yet! It's time that we took a new look at poop and pee. What we flush away today was precious in the past. People used human and animal waste for washing and beauty treatments and to make things such as gunpowder, leather, and medicines. Even now, it can help feed us, shelter us, and heat our homes. Turn the page to see what amazingly useful things you can do with pee and poop.

Kidneys

Stomach

Small intestine

Large intestine

Bladder

MANURE FOR
HEALTHIER PLANTS

LEATHER

BELL

POOP PRODUCTION

Poop is what is left over from what you eat. Your stomach churns food and adds natural chemicals, so you can absorb its nutrients in your small intestine. Your large intestine turns poop from a soup into a firmer paste. Pee makes a shorter journey. Your kidneys produce pee, and your bladder stores it.

POOP EMPORIUM

THE POOP CREW

LUCKY CHARMS

BEAUTY PRODUCTS

MEDICINES

BRICKS

EXPLOSIVES

WATER

ENVELOPES

YOUR GUIDES
On this pee and poop tour, you'll need a guide. Well, five actually. Meet the Poop Crew! Sidney Sewers (rat), Buzz (bluebottle), Pecker (pigeon), Roly (dung beetle), and "Sniffer" Jenkins (dog) will show you around.

TINNED ARTIST'S POOP-REDUCED

WHÂT'S IN WÂSTE?
Pee is mostly water. Just one-twentieth of it is made of salt, plus 70 chemicals that our bodies produce as waste. Poop is three-quarters water, too. Most of the rest is dead bacteria from the intestines, or undigested food. There are also small amounts of fats, minerals, and proteins.

Water

Bacteria

Fats   Proteins

Undigested food

Minerals

GÂTHERING GOLD

There's money in the sewer! What we flush down the toilet makes valuable fertilizer. As manure, poop helps food plants grow in farm fields. Before chemical fertilizers became available in the 1800s, poop was called "night soil" and was collected after dark. "Night soil men" gathered it from city sewers and pits before selling it to farms and markets. This trade continues in a few places and may expand as the rising cost of fertilizers forces farmers to use manure again.

STINKY MÂRKETS

Night soil men sold their poop products at markets. When Spanish explorers visited Tenochtitlan (now Mexico City) in 1519, they saw a night soil market. Chinese and Japanese cities also had markets, often near harbors, where night soil boats could be unloaded.

NIGHT SOIL COLLECTION

London night soil men worked in teams of four, always after midnight. The holeman climbed into the sewer and filled a bucket with sludge. The ropeman hauled it up, and two tubmen emptied it into a cart. Their jobs were considered so gross that they earned double the wage of a skilled worker.

WHÂT'S IT WORTH?

City sewage was not the best manure. A 10th-century writer claimed that pigeon dung was better for farming. After people's poop, the most valuable poop came from donkeys, goats, sheep, cattle, pigs, and then horses. Even humans were unequal: in 18th-century Japan, the poop of a rich samurai warrior was twice as valuable as that of a poor family.

HUMANURE
Spreading pee and poop on farms and gardens is kinder to the environment than washing away sewage. In regions without sewers, engineers have begun to install composting lavatories, which produce "humanure." Composting gets rid of bad smells and harmful germs.

LORDING IT UP
In medieval England, a wealthy lord had the right to fold (fence in) all the sheep and cattle on his land, so that their droppings enriched only his fields. Poorer people, who needed the manure more, hated this rule, which was called a "folding right."

FERTILIZER ISLAND
Using night soil as fertilizer ended in the mid-19th century with the discovery of guano—the fertile, dry droppings of seagulls and bats. The Pacific island of Nauru was once a guano mountain. Its mining made the islanders rich, but ruined their home.

HUMAN

DONKEY

GOAT

SHEEP

PIG

HORSE

GARDEN GROWERS

Hauled from city streets and smelly stables, night soil and manure have helped crops grow tall and strong for years. Pee and poop contain chemicals that plants need for growth, and they make the soil lighter, too. Farmers have been boosting their crops with manure for more than 10,000 years—but by the 1800s, gardeners had found many more ingenious uses for what they just called "muck."

READY SPREADY GO!

Found in fresh manure, the chemical ammonia is strong enough to turn leaves brown, so farmers and gardeners compost (rot) manure for at least six months before spreading it onto soil. Dung heats up quickly when it rots, so heaps are kept small to stop them from bursting into flames.

PINEAPPLE PITS

Gardeners used the heat of rotting dung to pamper delicate plants. Pineapples usually flourish only in tropical areas, but by surrounding pots with "hot beds" of rotting dung, gardeners in chilly northern Europe could grow the fruit.

HOT HATCHERS

Hatching eggs normally requires a mother hen's warm belly or an expensive heated incubator (hatching box). Instead, thrifty farmers used to put eggs in straw-filled barrels and warm them with rotting dung. That was hatching on the cheep!

WHÂT MITE HÂVE BEEN

Archaeologists have shown the importance of manure in farming by counting the remains of crops and tiny insects called dung mites. The Inca—Peru's ancient people—fertilized their corn fields with llama dung—the home and food of these tiny dung mites. In 2,700-year-old mud, corn and mite numbers matched, proving that more dung makes more corn.

MUSHROOM MIRÂCLE

Woods and fields have always been a source of delicious mushrooms. However, in the 1600s, French farmers found that growing them on dung heaps in dark caves or sheds was quicker than gathering them from the wild. This method is also used today to farm some supermarket mushrooms.

NÂME CHÂNGE

Today, sewage is a dirty word, and many people don't want to spread night soil on their fields or gardens. As a result, wastewater engineers now refer to sewage as "biosolids." Composted and harmless, biosolids even fertilize the lawn of the White House.

THE HUNT IS ON

On the trail of wild beasts, a piece of pristine poop provides as much information as a footprint. Skilled trackers call animal poop "scat." Its size, shape, smell, color, squishiness, and undigested food content are all valuable clues. Together, they can tell a hunter which animal dropped the deposit, how big the beast was, what it enjoyed for lunch, and how recently the poop was passed.

A MEDIEVAL HUNT

Hunting was the sport of kings in Europe during the Middle Ages (about A.D. 1000–1500). While the royal party had a picnic, humble trackers went in search of game to hunt. They prized any "fewmets" (scat) they found, because they could take it to their noble masters.

THE HARBORER'S JOB

The scat specialist on the hunt was the harborer. He put any fewmets he found in his shirt or hunting horn and then returned to the hunting party. There he presented the poop to his lady, usually at the beginning of a meal. By carefully studying the scat, the noblemen decided which beast to hunt.

WORD OF WARNING!

Be aware that scat can spread diseases and parasites. If you track animals and handle their scat, always wash your hands with soap and water right afterward.

MODERN TRACKING

Today, few people feed themselves by hunting and killing animals, but tracking skills are still valuable. On game reserves, rangers rely on scat to lead visitors to wildlife they want to see and photograph. Soldiers also learn tracking as a survival skill in remote regions.

ENDÂNGERED SPECIES

If animals are too rare or too shy to spot in the wild, scientists use scat to trace and count them. In the North Atlantic, fewer than 400 right whales survive. Detection dogs on boats sniff out whale scat, so biologists can check the whales' health.

Goose

Coyote

Rabbit

Rat

WHÂT'S THÂT SCÂT?

Puzzled about who left that pile of poop in your yard? Wildlife books can help you identify four-legged visitors, but a session with a local wildlife trust will be more "hands-on." These lifelike plastic samples can't help you recognize telltale odors, but at least you can carry them in your pocket for side-by-side comparisons.

SCENT OR STINK?

For animals, pee and poop smells are like a TV game show—with life-or-death prizes! Creatures use their powerful noses to detect danger or desire. They flee from the droppings of bigger, hungrier species and pick up on the signals that show an attractive mate is nearby. We humans have learned to use animal scents and stinks to lure the desirable and repel the dangerous.

ÂNIMÂL ÂTTRÂCTION

For a hungry fly, the smell of fresh poop signals "Dinner is served!" Many mammals have scent glands in their bladders and guts. When they are looking for a mate, these produce chemicals called pheromones, which the opposite sex find difficult to resist.

SCÂREDY-CÂTS

Determined cats can dig up a yard faster than its owner can repair it. Gardeners fight back with the help of the cat's fierce jungle cousins. *Silent Roar* cat repellent contains extract of lion poop. Its smell has cats running for safety.

DUNG DISGUISE

Even clean humans smell strong to animals, so getting dirty makes a good disguise. Some 19th-century African elephant hunters smeared themselves with elephant dung. The smelly camouflage meant that they could move unnoticed through a herd and spear them.

LIGHTING A SMUDGE

Poop was used to keep away midges and mosquitoes long before scientists invented chemical insect repellents. Missouri Native Americans, Chinese people, and Egyptian people all lit dung fires when these tiny pests plagued them. European explorers copied them, calling a dung fire a "smudge."

DANGER ZONE

If you have ever walked a male dog, you will have seen animal smells in action. Each time he lifts his leg to pee, your pet is leaving a message that he is the boss around there. Other species find such smells a threat and may avoid territory marked with pee or poop.

REINDEER ROUND-UP

The northern peoples of Canada, Alaska, and Siberia once tamed wild reindeer using pee. As the deer craved the salty taste of pee, herders laid long lines of it to round them up. This liking for pee makes tame deer a hazard for people peeing in the snow: the deer come running to drink it—and they are big!

DOWNSTREAM DIAGNOSIS

Eat a rotten prawn, and you'll get a fast lesson in diagnosis (identifying illness). Food poisoning changes the urgency of your bathroom visits, and it's one of many complaints that affect your pee and poop. Medieval doctors combined uroscopy (studying pee) with astrology for a diagnosis that was no better than guesswork. Urine tests are still common, but they are now more scientific and accurate.

A PEE CHART

In the past, doctors judged a patient's health by comparing pee samples with a color chart like this one. Here's an example diagnosis: "Urine that is thick, reddish, and milky shows that there is gout in the upper parts of the body." Whatever the color, the treatment was often the same: cutting open a vein to drain blood.

URINE TEST

What does my pee say about me? A change in appearance and flavor can hint at sickness. Blood in pee suggests the presence of a kidney stone (crystals of pee in the bladder). Foam may be a sign of kidney damage, and diabetes gives pee a sweet flavor. Laboratory tests reveal much more, including pregnancy, bladder infections, jaundice, and thyroid problems.

YOU MUST BE CROAKING!

In the 1960s, doctors injected live frogs with women's pee to see if they were expecting a baby. Pregnant women's pee contains hormones that can make frogs lay eggs. Today, frogs are not needed: women pee on strips that change color if they are pregnant.

BOTTLING IT UP

Doctors poured pee into special bottles to sniff, taste, and look at it. These uroscopy flasks had thin walls so that the glass did not disguise the color of the contents. The flasks became a symbol of the medical profession.

Eating beets turns your pee pink: try it!

1. Small, hard, and lumpy
2. Lumpy, but shaped like a sausage
3. Sausage-shaped, but with a cracked surface
4. Smooth and shaped like a snake or sausage
5. Soft pieces, but with clear edges
6. Fluffy, mushy bits with ragged edges
7. Watery and completely liquid

BRISTOL STOOL SCALE

How do you measure poop? For doctors treating gut diseases, it is a serious question. They use the Bristol Stool Scale: a guide to hardness, ranging from constipation (type 1) through normal (3 or 4) to diarrhea (7).

DOCTOR DUNG

For *sunus*, the doctors of ancient Egypt, dung and droppings were drugs. Their pills used poop from lions, gazelles, houseflies, ostrich, crocodiles, and other animals. Though *sunus'* ideas were mostly mistaken, folk remedies ever since have included poop and pee. Poop may even have a future in modern medicine. Physicians transplant it to heal gut problems that resist other treatments (see page 17).

CROCODILE

HOUSEFLY

GAZELLE

OSTRICH

LION

EGYPTIAN PHARMACY
About 3,500 years ago, Egyptian medicine was the best in the world, but *sunus* knew little about what made us sick. They guessed that devils and spirits caused diseases. To drive them out of a patient's body, they put poop into their prescriptions.

PEE WOUND WASH
Aztec warriors in ancient Mexico peed on sword wounds to clean them. Urine from a healthy person is sterile (does not contain germs). It is a safer wound wash than water from a muddy pool. Even today, some soldiers are taught to pee on wounds in an emergency.

FOLK MEDICINE

Medical science began to replace magic and superstition 300 years ago, but some people continued using toilet pharmacy. In 18th-century Pennsylvania, German immigrants drank a tea made from "sheep cherries" (sheep droppings) when they caught measles.

PEE IN THE AYURVEDA

This Indian medical tradition recommends urine as a cure. After drinking it for eight months, patients have a golden glow. Eight years of drinking urine makes patients live forever, and after ten years they can fly like birds! These claims are now widely regarded as false.

FECAL TRANSPLANTS

If the helpful bacteria in our guts die, a supergerm called *Clostridium difficile* can take over—with deadly results. In an experimental new treatment called fecal transplant, doctors inject a solution into patients' bottoms. The solution is made from healthy poop.

MÂKING Â SPLÂSH

No soap? Try washing with pee! Stale pee contains ammonia, a type of detergent that washes out grease. Before soap was invented, the first stage in washing clothes was often to soak them in a bucket of pee. In ancient Rome, 2,000 years ago, pee was so valuable that it was collected from public toilets. There was even a tax on urine: some of the money from the sale of pee—for washing, dyeing, and other chemical processes—went to the Roman government.

SHORTENED JÂRS
On street corners in Roman cities stood pottery jars for men to pee into. They were called *dolia curta* (shortened jars) because they were cut down to make them convenient for even the shortest Roman to use. Stinky slaves regularly collected the contents.

DYEING WITH INDIGO

Indigo is a beautiful blue dye that does not dissolve in water. But it does dissolve in stale pee, changing in color to yellow. Dyers soak plain cloth in the "urine pot." When they pull it out, the cloth dramatically turns bright blue as the air reacts with the indigo.

THE FULLER STORY

The contents of each *dolia curta* ended up here, at the fuller's workshop. Fullers processed cloth, but they also took in laundry, such as the togas that Roman citizens wore. Fullers threw the laundry into a big trough and filled it with pee and water.

SAILORS' SHIRTS

Soap doesn't work in salt water, so seamen on sailing ships saved up "chamber lye" (a polite name for pee) and soaked their shirts in it. To rinse clothes, they used precious drinking water or rainwater. Clothes rinsed in seawater never dry well.

A SMELLY TAX

When first-century Roman emperor Vespasian decided to put a tax—the *vectigal urinae*—on the pee that the fullers collected, his son Titus complained that it was disgusting. His father threw him a gold coin and asked, "Does the money smell bad?"

DIRTY WORK

The wealthy fuller didn't actually do the laundry. Instead, he got his slaves to do the dirty work. They climbed in the trough and stepped on the clothes underfoot. Lots of rinsing in fresh water followed—nobody wants to wear a toga that smells of pee!

DÂNGEROUS DUNG

What's brown, smells, and can blow your hand off? It sounds like a bad joke, but in 16th-century Europe, exploding dung was a deadly serious issue. Guns were replacing bows and arrows on the battlefields. The gunpowder needed to fire them was scarce and expensive. The answer? Dig up the nearest dunghill!

Farmyards, sties, chicken coops, and animal pens were a rich source of saltpeter.

PRECIOUS POWDER

Making an explosion required fuel and an "oxidizer"—a chemical that supplies masses of oxygen. In gunpowder, the oxidizer was saltpeter, or "niter" (potassium nitrate). It was found in a crude form in pee and poop. Saltpetermen made a pile of dung and poured pee onto it for months, until white crystals appeared on the surface. They checked, by licking them, that the crystals were of saltpeter, which had a "cold" taste. Mixing the crystals with water and wood ash purified them. Then boiling down the liquid concentrated and dried the saltpeter.

This is how they made saltpeter in 1580. The long mounds are dung heaps. A lot of dung is needed to make just a little saltpeter.

MĀKING GUNPOWDER

Saltpeter alone didn't go "BANG!" To make it explosive, it had to be mixed with charcoal and with a yellow chemical called sulfur. The quantities of each were vital for a satisfying and noisy blast. Making the powder was dangerous work. Millers ground the three ingredients separately into a fine powder before carefully mixing them into gunpowder. Then they took great care to avoid igniting it. Iron tools often create sparks, so workers handled the powders using copper or wood tools and containers. Leather covered the factory floors, and workers wore special slippers. Despite these precautions, deadly explosions were common.

The correct proportions for making gunpowder:

Charcoal:
3 parts

Sulfur:
2 parts

Saltpeter:
15 parts

SĀLTPETERMEN

Officials called "the king's saltpetermen" collected the dung needed to make gunpowder. Special laws gave them the power to remove dung heaps, the floors of stables, and other poopy places. Everyone hated them because they took the manure that farmers needed to make their crops grow, and they never repaired the floors that they tore up.

The ladies of Selma may have peed into a pot like this (left), decorated with a picture of a hated northern general.

PEE INTO POWDER

When America's southern states fought the North in the country's civil war, they soon ran short of gunpowder. As a result, an official in an Alabama town posted this advert in a local newspaper in 1862: "The ladies of Selma are respectfully requested to preserve all their chamber lye [urine] . . . . for the purpose of making niter. Wagons with barrels will be sent around for it." The message caused much amusement.

DING DONG DUNG

What's brown and sounds like a bell? It may be no more than a bad riddle, but the answer—"dung"—plays an important part in casting (shaping) bells. Nor is this the only use for pee and poop in the foundry. About 900 years ago, Viking swordsmiths made their finest blades using goose poop. Even today, pee-soaked soil adds a unique black finish to Bidriware—metal ornaments made from the stinky soil of a famous fortress.

MIXING LOÂM

Molds used in shaping bells are made from loam—a mixture of dung, clay, sand, and goat hair. The bell founders shape loam into the mold's two parts, forming the inside and outside.

PERFECT CÂSTING

To get the casting underway, bell makers melt metal at 1,650°F (900°C). They pour this liquid metal into the mold—a container the exact shape of the bell. Pouring the metal is the most skilled part of bell casting.

HEÂVY METÂL

As the metal flows into the mold, its intense heat burns away the dung that was mixed into the loam. This leaves tiny channels in the mold. The hot metal makes the air inside the mold swell suddenly. The channels created by the dung allow the expanding air to escape without cracking the mold.

Goat hair

Horse manure

Sand

SWORD SAGA

In a Viking saga (story), a blacksmith made his finest sword, named Mímungr, by feeding scraps of lesser swords to his geese. Then he added goose droppings to the metal that he melted to cast Mímungr. Scientists guess that traces of other chemicals in the goose dung really strengthened the sword.

QUENCHING DAMASCUS

Medieval blacksmiths hardened red-hot metal by quenching (cooling) it in water or pee. The best swords came from Damascus, where blacksmiths insisted on pee from red-headed boys. But they may have spread this story to hide the true secret of their superior blades.

Pouring molten metal into loam mold

BIDRIWARE

The Indian makers of this fancy metalware coat it with soil dug from the darkest corners of the walls of Bidar Fort. Visitors have peed in these spots for centuries, and chemicals in the rich, smelly soil instantly blacken the metal's surface.

LIBERTY BELL

When bell casting isn't perfect, the faults are not always obvious. The United States's Liberty Bell was cast in London, U.K. at the Whitechapel Bell Foundry. When it was rung in Philadelphia for the first time, a crack appeared in its side. Today—still cracked—it is more famous than any faultless American bell!

MIXING IT

Mud bricks are mostly made of . . . well, mud. But mud on its own cracks when it dries. Adobe builders mix in animal dung or straw to add strength and stop cracks. Dung contains fine fibers from undigested plants and also helps make the mud soft and easily molded.

DUNG IT YOURSELF

In some of the world's hot, dry places, builders rely on dung. It holds up roofs and keeps out the heat. Dung is a vital ingredient in muddy bricks called adobe. They were the first bricks ever made. They supported the ancient world's greatest structures, such as the famous walls of the city of Babylon, built more than 2,500 years ago. Adobe bricks are still used to create homes that are cool in the sun, but warm during chilly nights.

MAGIC MUD

To stick adobe bricks together, builders use more of the same type of mud. The walls they create are sturdy, but not very waterproof. Overhanging roofs of straw or iron sheeting stop rain from turning bricks back to mud.

MOLDING THE MUD

Mud bricks are molded—shaped—in a wooden frame. It is messy, slow, hard work. Newly molded bricks are left to dry for about three days. Then they are stacked for a month to harden before use.

SHIBÂM!

The world's first high-rise buildings were made from adobe bricks. About 500 of them still stand in the town of Shibâm in Yemen, Arabia. The tallest is 100 ft. (30m) high. Shibâm's unusual homes were built upward to protect their owners from warlike neighbors.

POOP PLÂSTER

Adobe buildings are coated with a mud-and-dung plaster to fill cracks and keep out the rain. Some adobe builders believe that adding horse pee to the plaster helps protect it from damage. "Neigh" way!

WÂTTLE ÂND DÂUB

Even in damp, northern Europe, dung makes a useful building material. Mixed with mud, it creates daub. This thick, brown coating is smeared on wattle-woven wooden panels that form the walls of traditional, wood-framed buildings.

BRICKS IN EGYPT

Tomb paintings from ancient Egypt show builders mixing and molding bricks. People with better jobs looked down on them. One wrote that the builders "work outside naked, kneading excrement [poop] to make bricks, then eating bread . . . without washing their hands."

TÂN YOUR HIDE

In the 1800s, people didn't need good eyesight to find a tannery—they just followed their nose. Turning animal skins into leather required a special, stinky ingredient—dog poop. It contains bacteria (tiny bugs) that made the leather soft and smooth. Tanners called this poop "pure," and collecting it from city streets was the job of the "pure finder."

PURE FINDERS

Collecting dog poop was a fairly good job! During the 1850s, in London, U.K., men who worked as pure finders were better paid than those who collected and sold rags and bones. Tanneries paid a shilling (7¢) for each bucket of pure, and this was enough to buy three large loaves.

TAKE THE BATE

To soften the very best leather, tanners soaked hides in "bate," a sloshy poop-mud. They made bate by tipping poop into a tub, adding water, and kneading it with their feet. Then they tossed in the hides (animal skins) and stepped on them for several hours.

HARD-WORKING DOGS

Street collections were not the only source of pure. Tanners also bought it from kennels, and many kept dogs themselves. The dogs worked hard for their keep. Besides supplying pure, they also tore the last strips of flesh from the animal hides before tanning could begin.

BALD BEGINNINGS
Scraping the skins with a blunt, curved knife removed any unwanted hair before the bating process.

INUIT TANNING

In America's frozen north, Inuit people tanned animal skins using pee, which they collected in ice troughs during the winter. Other Native American groups used pee in tanning, sometimes mixing it with crushed animal brains. Fat in the brains made the leather soft and supple.

WHITEOUT
Tanners paid more for white poop because it did not stain the leather. Dishonest pure finders cheated them by rolling regular, brown poop in ground-up chalk.

THE END RESULT

After bating, tanners washed the leather many times, but sometimes not enough to remove the smell of the pure. Leather dealers checked for this by sniffing or licking the hides they bought. This "trick of the trade" was no longer needed after chemical tanning replaced the bating process in the late 1800s.

MESSY MAKEOVER

Are you worth it? Do you deserve to be smothered in pee and poop? Of course you do! In search of beauty, anything goes. Skin and hair products have an ancient connection to the dung heap. Beauticians and barbers used pee and poop to lighten and whiten, to make hair grow, and also to make it fall out. Even today, some cosmetics include urea and ammonia, which are found in pee.

JENKINS

BIONDA

CROC SKIN
In his medical textbook of the A.D. first century, Greek pharmacist Dioscorides recommended face cream containing crocodile dung "for coloring the face and making it shine." He warned of fakes, made from the poop of rice-fed starlings.

Today, a Japanese company sells a nightingale-poop face cream.

BOTTLE BLONDE
For the women of 16th-century Venice, blonde was beautiful. They combed *bionda* (a mix of lemon juice and stale pee) into their hair. Then they lay in the sun, shading their pale skin with the cut-off rim of a hat. Together, sunshine and *bionda* acted as a bleach to lighten the hair.

HANDS DOWN
German doctor Johann Wecker wrote a popular beauty manual in the 1600s. One of his top tips was smearing fingernails with a mix of "arsenic and dog turd" in order to lighten them.

WHÂLE WÂSTE

Tiny amounts of ambergris give a unique scent to the finest perfumes. Gray and waxy, ambergris floats into the ocean in the poop of sperm whales. Washed ashore, it's as valuable as gold.

MOUSE-TÂCHES

During the 1700s, German men who longed for droopy mustaches were advised to smear mouse droppings under their noses. The same remedy was supposed to cure dandruff, too.

NIGHTLY REFILLS

Doves, donkeys, camels, cows, swallows, mice, cats, rats, rabbits, and goats have all provided the raw material for hair and skin care. But human pee was always popular in times past—perhaps because there was always a pot of it under the bed.

TRÂDITIONÂL TÂTTOOS

Inuit people created their own tattoos using a mixture of pee and soot. They pulled a thread through the mix and then used a needle to pass it under the skin. It may be possible that urea, a natural chemical found in pee, helped stop the skin from getting infected.

BÂCKSIDE BUFFET

Poop on a plate? No thank you! It may sound sickening, but many rare and highly prized foods from around the world get their unusual flavors through being processed with dung. Drinking pee is more common. In fact, you probably drank some today, in your tap water. A few people go further, glugging down their own pee by the glass as a wacky health cure. Ice with that? Yes, please!

ICELAND
As winter draws in, Icelanders with smokehouses light a sheep dung fire and hang a leg of lamb above it. The smoked delicacy is called *Hangikjöt* ("hanging meat"). It's a popular Christmas treat.

INDONESIA
The world's most expensive coffee, *Kopi Luwak*, is made thanks to wild tree cats called palm civets. When these cats eat coffee berries, chemicals in their guts remove the bitterness of the beans inside. Workers collect the beans from civet droppings and then wash, dry, and roast them.

DRINKING URINE

In small amounts, fresh human urine is harmless and safe to drink. It is even a traditional medicine in India (see page 17). Those in the West who drink their own pee, for its supposed health benefits, say that it tastes better when chilled. Cheers!

WATER RECYCLING

Worldwide, most city water contains what was once pee. In Windhoek, Namibia, tap water is made from recycled sewage. The water authorities purify river water, which includes the sewage from towns upstream.

FRANCE

A traditional French hot drink, *chocolat ambré*, contains ground-up ambergris. This precious flavor, which is also used in perfume, is harvested from sperm whale poop.

AMERICA

During the 1700s, California Native Americans who ate the cactus fruit *pitahaya* could not digest the tiny seeds. Collected from their poop, the seeds were delicious when roasted and ground up.

MOROCCO

Moroccan goats climb argan trees to eat the fruit, but they cannot digest the stones inside. Herders pick the stones from goat dung. They crush the pits to make tasty argan oil, which is sold for cooking and cosmetics.

MUCK, MYTH, & MAGIC

Embrace the magic power of poop! People from the past believed that it brought good luck, so they worshiped dung gods and goddesses. It's easy to see why. Their lives depended on crops. Pee and poop enriched the soil, keeping crops growing and hungry mouths fed. Today, just a few cultures celebrate the tradition of poop worship. But many of us still say "that means good luck!" when a bird poops on our shoulder.

STERCUTIUS

This ancient Roman god of poop was connected with manuring the soil. He got his name from *stercus*, the word for dung in the Latin language that Romans spoke. Greeks worshiped him as Saturn, the god of agriculture.

SACRED SCARAB

Ancient Egyptians worshiped a black beetle because it rolled dung balls—just as the god Ra rolled the sun across the sky each day. In one of his forms, Ra appears as a scarab (dung) beetle.

CLOACINA

This Roman coin shows the sewer godess Cloacina. Her shrine was next to the *Cloaca Maxima*, the great drain that she protected. Rome's sewage flowed down it into the Tiber River.

LUCKY LANDING

Many superstitious people think that bird poop landing on clothes brings luck. This belief may have begun with *stercomancy*— the art of telling people's fortunes by studying the seeds found in dung.

KUMÂLÂK

On the patterned *kumalak* playing cloth, shamans (holy men) of Kazakhstan used to tell villagers' fortunes using 41 dried sheep droppings. Sadly, modern *kumalak* sets use 41 counters or beads instead.

HOLY COW!

Hindus consider the cow to be a sacred animal, and the cow god *Kamadhenu* can grant any wish. At the January harvest festival in India, girls honor him with *Gobbemmalu*—brightly decorated cow droppings.

KIN NO UNKO

Japanese people buy gold-coated *kin no unko* (golden poop) charms to share in the luck that the toilet gods promise (see right). But they are also enjoying a pun (a word joke). In Japanese, the words "poop" and "luck" start with the same "oon" sound.

TOILET GOD

Benjo-Kami is a Japanese spirit from the Shinto religion who lives in and protects the family toilet. Singer Kana Uemura made the god more famous in 2011 with a hit song about cleaning her grandma's toilet!

Dinosaur coprolites are prehistoric monsters: a *Tyrannosaurus rex* dropping can be 20 in. (50cm) long! Within these chunky fossils, pieces of bone, teeth, wood, leaves, seeds, fish scales, and shells survive to teach us about dino dining. Burrows in coprolites can also help identify prehistoric dung beetles.

Dinosaur coprolite

POOP OF THE PAST

For scientists who study the past, there's a clue in the poop. We can learn what dinosaurs ate from what passed through their guts. Dropped more than 100 million years ago, dino dumps hardened into rocklike coprolites (dung stones). Poop can tell us a lot about recent history. By digging up our ancestors' toilets, archaeologists have made us rethink our ideas about how humans spread across the globe.

Microscope

Diamond-tipped saw

DUNG DISCOVERY

Medieval people called coprolites "bezoar stones," and believed that they cured a variety of medical problems. English fossil hunters William Buckland and Mary Anning were the first to guess what they really were, and Buckland named them coprolites in 1829.

PALEOSCATOLOGISTS

To look inside a dinosaur coprolite, paleoscatologists (the scientists who study them) cut off thin slices using a diamond-tipped saw (left) and smooth them flat and shiny. A microscope (far left) magnifies the specimens, which are so thin that light shines right through them.

CAVE POOP BREAKTHROUGH

American archaeologist Dennis Jenkins used 14,300-year-old human poop from a cave in Oregon, to show that Asian people reached North America 1,200 years earlier than people had previously thought (see page 46) in the poop revealed the cave dwellers' origins.

Dennis Jenkins

PEOPLE'S POOP

You could break a toe on a dinosaur coprolite, but the human version is more like something you may step in. Archaeologists restore the original texture and smell of people's poop by soaking it in cleaning solutions. What they find inside can reveal the diet of the person, indicating, for example, whether they were rich or poor.

FLÂMING FUEL

On the treeless plains of the American West, wood was too valuable to make into fires. To cook and stay warm, settlers burned buffalo poop instead. With 60 million buffalo, each one dropping three bucketfuls a day, there was no shortage. Cowboys didn't invent dung fires. They copied the ways of Native Americans. Even today, dung warms the poor and cooks their food in places where other fuel is scarce.

MEÂDOW MUFFINS

Settlers had many names for buffalo dung. "Meadow muffins" was the most polite. The French called dung "cow wood." Each fall, settler families spent at least two weeks picking up meadow muffins to burn during the winter. Snow then made collection impossible until the spring thaw.

WOMEN'S WORK

Collecting fuel was traditionally women's work, and popular songs made fun of women who were too proud for the job. In the words of one, ". . . look at her now with a pout on her lips; as daintily, with her fingertips; she picks for the fire some buffalo chips."

BURNING BRIGHT

Dung burned with a stinking smoke if it was damp, but dry dung burned well in a good wind. Though a dung fire never got very hot, it had one huge advantage over wood. Dung did not spit sparks that could burn clothes or set fire to a tepee or a settler's wagon.

CAMEL CRAZY

As a desert animal, the camel has to conserve water. Its guts squeeze every drop of water from digested food, so camel poop burns on a fire without needing to be dried first. Wherever camels graze, their owners collect the dung for fires. This girl is carrying a bowlful of dung at India's Pushkar camel fair.

Dung was burned regularly in order to get campfires sizzling in the American West.

POOP PROBLEMS

Dung is not a perfect fuel. Its smoky flame creates indoor air pollution and can cause lung problems. Plus, a dung fire is like burning food to cook food. If alternative fuels were available, dung could fertilize fields instead, making crops grow better.

IT'S A GAS

One terrifying night in 1847, a giant explosion shook London's foggy streets. According to reports, a "vast flame" roared from a sewer, spreading "an unbearable stench." The cause was the gas given off by rotting pee and poop. Today, we harvest sewer gas, or "biogas," which is an environmentally friendly alternative to fossil fuels such as coal and oil.

ANUDDER PROBLEM
Biogas forms in a cow's guts. Using collectors such as this balloon, scientists guess that the world's cows make 100 million tons of methane gas each year. If we could harvest it, this could help replace fossil fuels. But we can't, so cow farts continue to warm our climate.

A pipe takes toilet waste to the digester. Garden waste can be shoveled in, too.

FEEDING TIME
Biogas can be made from all kinds of waste, but to make lots of gas requires lots of waste. In home biogas systems, the toilet feeds into the digester (see page 39). However, big commercial systems use waste from farms: pee and poop from cows, pigs, and hens.

EXPLODING SEWERS
Sewer explosions regularly rocked city streets in the past. They happened most often when workers who were cleaning or repairing sewers struck matches or lit candles. Sewers rarely explode today because they have vents that release gases, so that the gases do not build up to dangerous levels.

ÂNAEROBIC DIGESTER

To turn pee and poop into useful biogas, microbes (tiny bacteria) have to digest it. They make more gas if there is no air, so biogas digesters are built to keep out the atmosphere. This is why they are called "anaerobic" digesters: anaerobic means "free of air."

A do-it-yourself digester at work

BURNING BIOGÂS

The gas from a backyard digester burns well in an ordinary cooking stove. However, gas from big commercial plants is purified before it is fed into the pipes leading to homes. It may also be burned at the plant to generate electricity.

BÂCKYÂRD BIOGÂS

You, too, could power your stove with poop! All you need to do is fill a concrete-lined tank with sewage. A big plastic membrane is used to keep air out and gas in. A pipe takes the gas to your house. China is a world leader in biogas energy, installing about four million of these family biogas units each year.

POOPER PÂPER

Making paper usually means crushing trees in giant machines. But there is an alternative way to get paper from plants: just feed them to hungry animals. The beasts' teeth and guts grind and digest the green plants. What is left of the meal emerges at the other end, ready to turn into soft, smooth paper sheets.

POO PECKERS

Mammals that eat plants have special guts to digest tough leaves, but a lot of what goes in their mouths still comes out unchanged. Birds and insects know this, and flock to fresh poo to pick tasty morsels from the fibres.

Elephants produce a wheelbarrow-load of dung each day.

Dung is washed and boiled for several hours.

Simple mixers make the fibers shorter.

These dung balls contain equal amounts of fiber.

POOP CÂNOE

The Welsh makers of Sheep Poo Paper have found a novel use for it. Layered with beeswax and waterproof resin, it covers a homemade canoe. The daring canoeists plan to paddle their boat from the U.K. to France to raise money for charity.

PERFECT PÂPER

In the digestive system of elephants, half the fiber that they eat passes right through their guts. Because it contains so much fiber, elephant poop is the ideal raw material for paper. Processing removes smells, cleans and sterilizes the plant fibers, and separates them from unwanted material.

BÂMBOO POOP

China's Chengdu panda breeding center once had a giant problem: disposing of two tons of panda poop a day. But now they make it into paper to raise money for the center. Pandas digest just 20 percent of their bamboo diet, and the paper smells of bamboo.

Wetting each ball spreads out the fibers, and sifting through a fine mesh creates a soggy paper sheet.

Drying sheets in the sun creates the finished paper.

WRITE-ON!

Poop paper looks and smells like any other good-quality, handmade paper. You can write, draw, or print on it. Although poop paper is an expensive novelty, making it helps support communities by providing jobs and attracting tourist visits.

BRUSHSTROKES

For the world's very first artists, painting with pee was simply practical: it was always available in the dark caves where they worked. Today's painters use pee and poop for more creative reasons. They know that these materials are more shocking than paint. They use them as a reminder of their culture and roots. Or they enjoy the joke of making priceless art from worthless stuff.

'CÂ-CÂ-CÂVE PÂINTINGS

Working more than 40,000 years ago, early artists painted elegant images of the beasts that they hunted. Instead of paint, they used mud in shades of red, yellow, brown, and black. To stick it to rocks, or to the walls and ceilings of caves, they needed some liquid, so many of them used pee.

ROMÂN REMÂINS

Belgian artist Wim Delvoye built *Cloaca* as a "useless machine" to show how pointless modern life is. Named after the Roman sewer (see page 32), *Cloaca* is an artificial gut. Food that goes in at one end emerges at the other as lifelike poop.

MUCKY MONKS

Illuminated manuscripts (painted books) of the Middle Ages hide a smelly secret. The monks who created them got their materials from their monastery's *reredorter* (communal toilet). Urine contains a chemical that, when heated, set the books' colors or made them brighter.

MASKING THE POOP

The Gurunsi people of west Africa's Burkina Faso make and paint masks that are world famous and highly valuable. The masks represent a range of spirits and animals. Gurunsi artists create white paint from lizard poop, which they collect out of the animals' burrows.

POO INTO MOO!

British sculptor Sally Matthews was brought up on a farm, where there was never a shortage of cow dung. She used eight buckets of it—along with sheep's wool and wire—to build this amazingly lifelike cow. Thanks to the materials, it even *smells* like a cow.

...AND BEYOND...

If you have read this far, you will know the value of pee and poop. We need to use them wisely because our planet's resources are shrinking. In space, astronauts already practice what we must all learn—drinking each and every drop of water time after time. On Earth below, inventive pee and poop projects show the way forward.

Space toilets are cunningly designed to vacuum up the weightless pee and poop.

The recycled pee that astronauts drink is purer than our tap water.

FREEZE-DRIED PEE
Some space missions just dumped pee and poop, and this sewage still orbits Earth today. Colliding with it can do as much damage to a spacecraft as a truck moving at expressway speed.

RECYCLING URINE
The risk of crashing into their own bodily waste is not the only reason why astronauts have been recycling it since 2008: shipping water up to a space station costs $11,000 a glass! The spacecraft's water recovery system filters and purifies not only pee, but washing water and sweat as well.

IOWA MANURE

It takes a lot of energy to make fertilizers, and as oil prices rise, so too do farmers' costs. Farmers in Iowa are saving money—and the environment—by replacing chemical fertilizers with traditional manure.

THE POWER OF POOP

Making methane (see page 38) is not just about backyard biogas burps. At Didcot in Oxfordshire, U.K., a shiny new anaerobic digester is supplying gas to about 200 homes. It is powered by waste from the region's sewage system.

NEW TOILETS

In this slum in Brazil there is no proper sewer. Worldwide, four out of ten families do not have decent toilets. Inventors are competing to build cheap toilets that don't waste water and to safely convert poop into fuel and fertilizer.

BOLIVIAN CLEAN-UP

Poop stops poisons from reaching the water supply. In Bolivia, the Andes mountains' streams are too polluted to drink. But passing the water through dropping-filled mines are to the mineral waste. A lot

DIRTY WORDS

adobe
A dried mud brick.

ambergris
A gray material produced in the guts of whales and used in food and perfume.

archaeologist
A scientist who learns about the past by digging up the remains and possessions of people from long ago.

arsenic
A poisonous, metal-like chemical.

bacteria (plural of bacterium)
Minute creatures that cause decay or diseases in plants and animals.

bamboo
A type of giant grass that grows quickly.

biogas
A fuel gas produced by biological waste and sewage.

biosolid
Sewage made harmless and spread as a fertilizer.

bladder
The organ in an animal's body that collects and stores pee.

camouflage
A pattern on the surface of an animal, building, or vehicle that makes it less easy to see.

charcoal
A black, smokeless fuel made by heating wood.

climate change
The way that our planet's climate is warming, and becoming less easy to predict, caused by the burning of fossil fuels.

concentrate
To make a solution stronger by reducing the amount of liquid.

coprolite
Fossilized animal dung—for example, that of a dinosaur.

dandruff
Flakes of dead skin that fall from the scalp (surface of the head).

decay
The breaking down and rotting of dead things.

diabetes
A medical condition that makes people store sugar in their bodies, causing thirst and constant peeing.

dissolve
To mix something solid into a liquid so that no particles of the solid can be seen.

distillation
Separation—by heating—of a mixture of liquids that boil at different temperatures.

DNA
A biological code, stored in living cells, that controls how plants and animals live, grow, and reproduce.

donor
A person who gives something, such as a part of their body, to another person.

dye
A colored substance that can change the color of materials that it mixes with.

fertilizer
A material that makes soil richer, so that plants can grow in it better.

fortunetelling
Predicting what will happen to someone in the future.

fossil fuels
Fuels extracted from the planet, such as gas, coal, and oil. These materials formed hundreds of millions of years ago from the remains of ancient forests.

fuller
A worker who treats cloth, after it is woven, to clean and thicken it.

gunpowder
An explosive powder.

guts
The digestive system of an animal, passing through the whole length of its body.

herder
Someone who looks after a group of farm animals.

hormone
A signaling chemical that moves around the body in fluids such as blood.

immigrant
Someone who leaves their homeland behind and goes to another country to start a new life.

jaundice
A condition of the liver that causes yellowing of the skin.

manure
Animal dung spread on soil to make it better for growing plants and crops.

mate
The partner that a person or animal chooses, with the aim of starting a family.

membrane
A thin layer or wall enclosing something, or keeping two different things apart.

microbe
Something other than a poison that causes diseases or bad health. A germ, basically.

Middle Ages
Also called medieval, the period of European history between ancient and modern times: approximately A.D. 1000–1500.

mold
A container shaped to enclose a hardening paste, such as mud, so that, when set, the paste takes the shape of the mold.

night soil
Solid human waste taken from toilets and streets at night.

orbit
To move in a circular path around Earth, without falling to the ground or flying off into space.

oxidizer
A substance that causes another substance to have a chemical reaction with oxygen.

paleoscatologists
Scientists who study preserved poop to learn about the lives of people or animals from the past.

pollution
Waste from human activity that harms air, soil, or water.

prehistoric
Something that existed or took place before recorded history began.

prescription
A form from a doctor asking a pharmacist to supply a healing drug.

repellent
Something unpleasant that makes an animal go away.

sacred
Having special importance in a religion.

saltpeter
A white, powdery chemical that, when mixed with many other substances and lit, makes them burn more quickly.

scat
The droppings of an animal.

sewage
Liquid and solid waste from the human gut and bladder.

sewer
A pipe for carrying sewage.

shrine
A small place for prayer and worship in a temple, home, or street.

sterile
Not containing any germs.

sunu
A doctor in ancient Egypt.

thyroid
An organ in the neck that produces growth hormones.

transplant
To move an organ or other material from one person's body to another's.

uroscopy
Looking at urine to try and identify an illness in a person or animal.

vent
An opening through which gases can escape.

INDEX

PICTURE CREDITS

The Publisher would like to thank the following for permission to reproduce their material. Every care has been taken to trace copyright holders. However, if there have been unintentional omissions or failure to trace copyright holders, we apologize and will, if informed, endeavor to make corrections in any future edition.

t = top; b = bottom; c = center; l = left; r = right

Cover Shutterstock/christil80884 and pages 6 Getty/SSPL; 7t Art Archive(AA)/Real Biblioteca de lo Escorial; 7b Alamy/MEPL; 9t Science Photo Library (SPL)/Power and Syred; 9b Shutterstock/Vacclav; 11t1 Getty AWL; 11tr Dr. Rosalind M. Roland D.V.M., Right Whale Conservation Medicine Program, New England Aquarium; 11ctl, ctr, bcl & bcr Acorn Naturalists, California; 13b Shutterstock/Andreas Gradin; 14 AA/University Library, Prague/Dagli Orti; 15tl FLPA/Pete Oxford/Minden; 15tr Jpbl301/wikipedia;17 SPL/Dr. Tony Brain, 19tl Superstock/Eye Ubiquitous; 19b Getty/de Agostini; 20 Heritage Images/Oxford Science Archive; 21 Alabama Department of Archives and History, Montgomery, Alabama; 23t Pictures From History; 23b Randhirreddy @ wik; 25ct Getty/Lonely Planet; 25lc Alamy/Paul Felix Photography; 25br AA/Dagli Orti; 26 Alamy/World History Archive; 27 AA/Kharbine-Tapabor Collection, Polas; 31 Alamy/ frans lemmens; 33t Alamy/RIA Novosti; 33cr Alamy/Tim Gainey; 34 SPL/Ted Kinsman; 35 Jim Barlow/University of Oregon; 37t Shutterstock/Jeremy Richards; 37b Getty/James L. Stanfield; 38 Corbis/Marcus Brindicci/Reuters; 40 www.SheepPooPaper.com; 41 Shutterstock/Hung Chung Chih; 42 With the kind permission of Wim Delvoye, Antwerp; 43t Alamy/Worldwide Picture Library; 43b Getty/Barcroft Media; 45tl Alamy/AGStockUSA; 45tr SPL/James King-Holmes/scitechimage; 45c Getty/Universal Pictures; 45bl Alamy/James Brunker.

The authors would also like to thank the following: Paul Barreau for clarifying an Internet myth about dung hurling at the Camel Cup races. Melanie Brown of Biophase for her advice on Bioremediation. Ian Chilvers for his help with art. Jean Smoke of HTI for her information on the company's remarkable water-filtering membranes. Professor Paul Younger of Newcastle University and Associate Professor Bod Nairn of the University of Oklahoma for their information concerning bioremediation and llama dung.